ENGLISH / AMERICAN SIGN LANGUAGE

THE Toddler's First 150 animal handbook

BY ASHLEY LEE

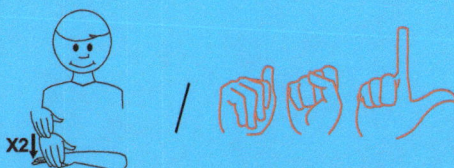

e ENGAGE BOOKS
VANCOUVER

1

e ENGAGE BOOKS

Mailing address
PO BOX 4608
Main Station Terminal
349 West Georgia Street
Vancouver, BC
Canada, V6B 4A1

www.engagebooks.com

Written by: Ashley Lee
Edited by: A.R. Roumanis
Illustrations by: Julian Rodriguez
Proofread by: Katherine Velliquette

FIRST EDITION / FIRST PRINTING

LIBRARY AND ARCHIVES CANADA CATALOGUING IN PUBLICATION

Lee, Ashley, 1995–, author
    The toddler's first 150 animal handbook
written by Ashley Lee ; edited by A.R. Roumanis.

Issued in print and electronic formats.
ISBN 978-1-77437-792-5 (hardcover)
ISBN 978-1-77437-742-0 (paperback)
ISBN 978-1-77437-391-0 (pdf)
ISBN 978-1-77437-392-7 (epub)
ISBN 978-1-77437-393-4 (kindle)

1. Animals—Juvenile literature
2. Vocabulary—Juvenile literature
3. American Sign Language—Vocabulary—Juvenile literature
I. Roumanis, A. R., editor
II. Title.

LCC QL49 .L442 2020 DDC J590—DC23
    C2020-027594-1 C2020-027595-X

4

BODY PARTS

6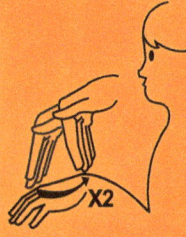

PETS

9

FARM

14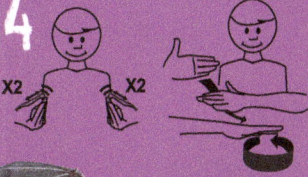

UNDERGROUND

16

FOREST

20

ARCTIC

22

OCEAN

28

GRASSLANDS

36

BUGS

40

EQUATOR

42

BIRDS

46

3 ACTIVITY

Nose

Paw

Tail

Feather

Ears

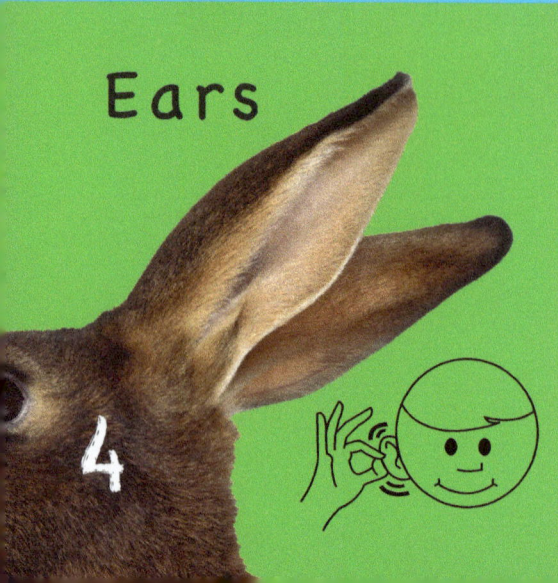

4

Fin

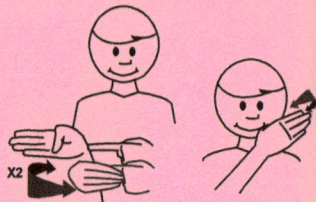

Claw

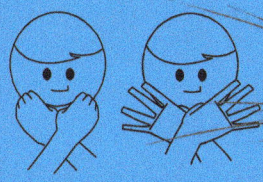

Whiskers

Antlers

Beak

Wing

Mane

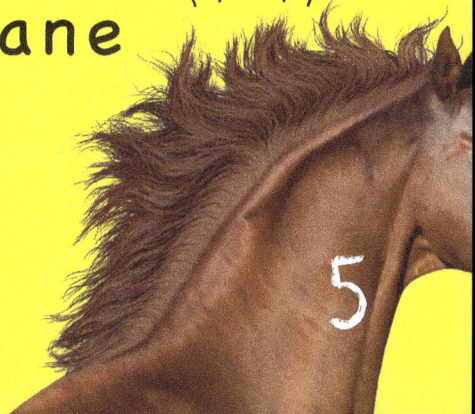

Pets

Cat

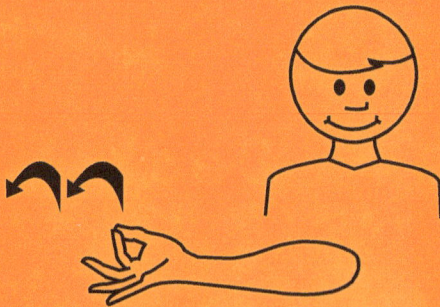

6 Ferret

Rabbit

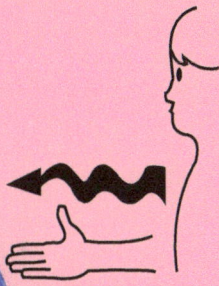

Fish

Guinea Pig

Hedgehog

Goldfish 7

Dog

Rat

8 Gerbil

Budgie

Farm

Pig

Horse

Pony 9

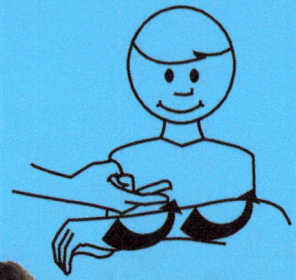

Donkey

Sheep

10 Emu

Cow

Chicken

Rooster

Turkey

Goose 11

Goat

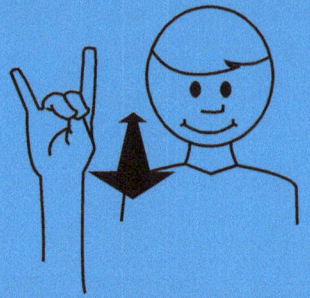

Llama

12 Duck

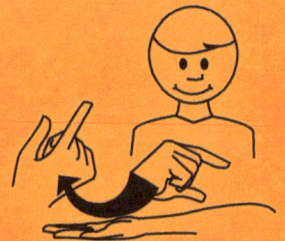

Guinea Fowl

Alpaca

Ostrich

Peacock

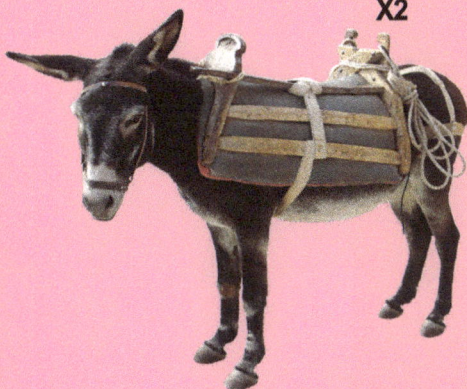

Mule 13

Underground

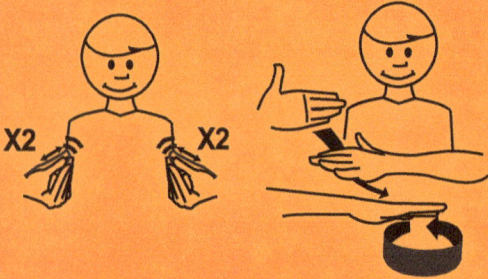

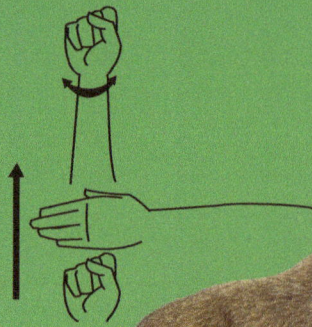

Groundhog

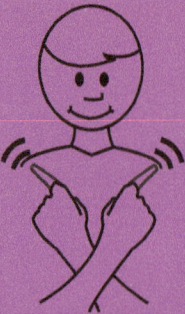

14   Bat

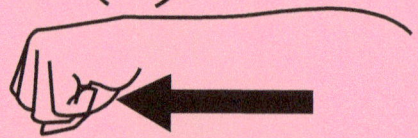

Ant

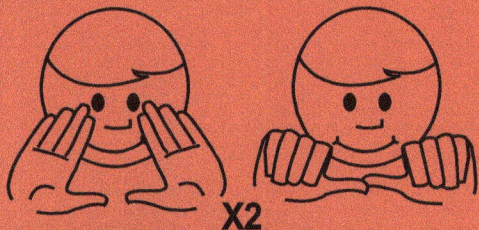

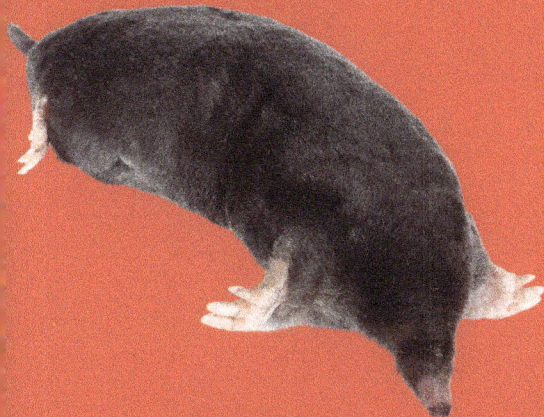

Mole

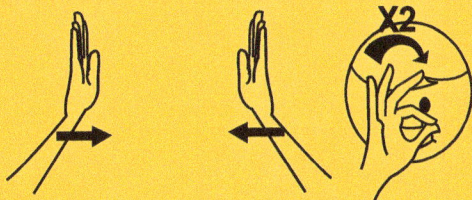

Fennec Fox

Worm

Badger 15

Forest

Cougar

16 Possum

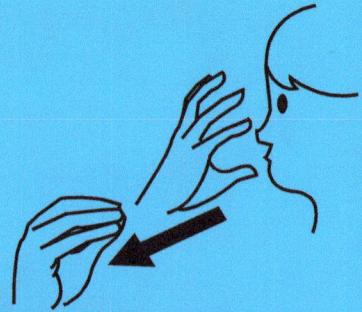

Wolf

Bear

Deer

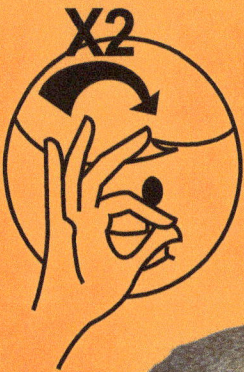

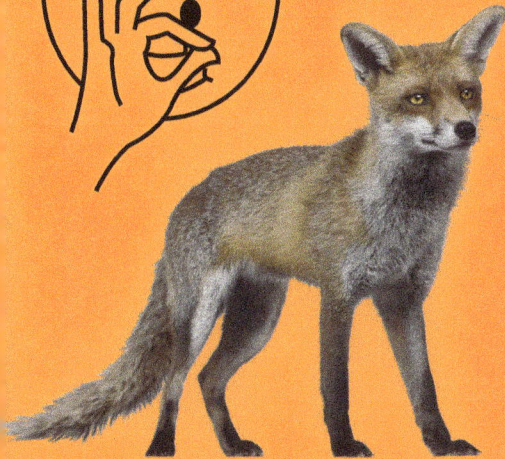

Fox

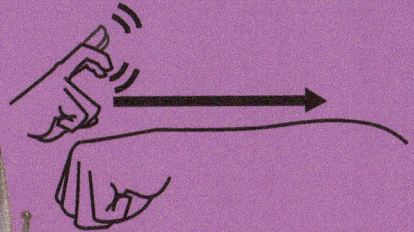

Snail 17

Toad

Eagle

18 Skunk

Porcupine

Racoon

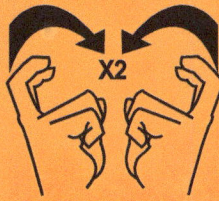

Chipmunk

Squirrel

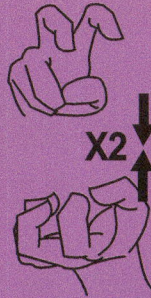

Beaver 19

Arctic

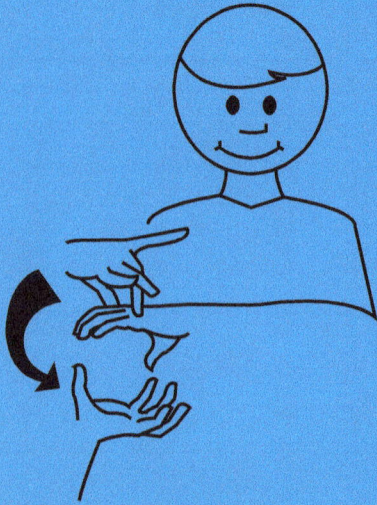

Snowy Owl

20 Sled Dog

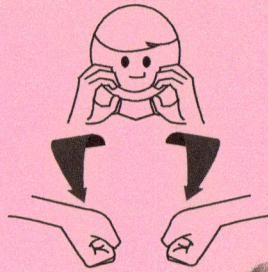

Walrus

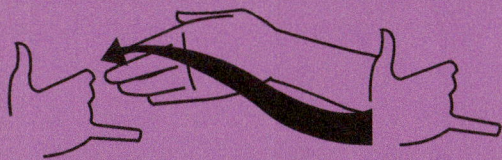

Orca

Reindeer

Polar Bear

Penguin 21

Ocean

Hammerhead Shark

22 Salmon

Otter

 **X2**

Crab

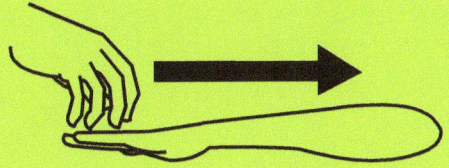

Hermit Crab

Shrimp

X2

Lobster 23

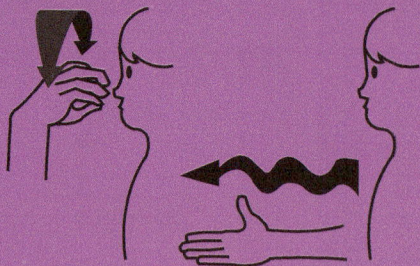

Clownfish

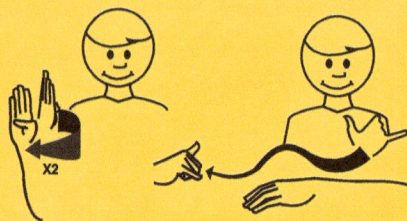

Blue Whale

24 Shark

Sea Lion

Sea Turtle

Seahorse

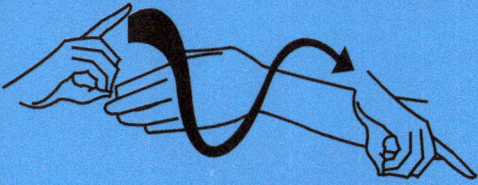

Dolphin

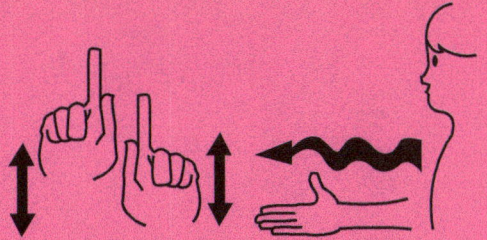

Starfish 25

Octopus

Clam

26 **Eel**

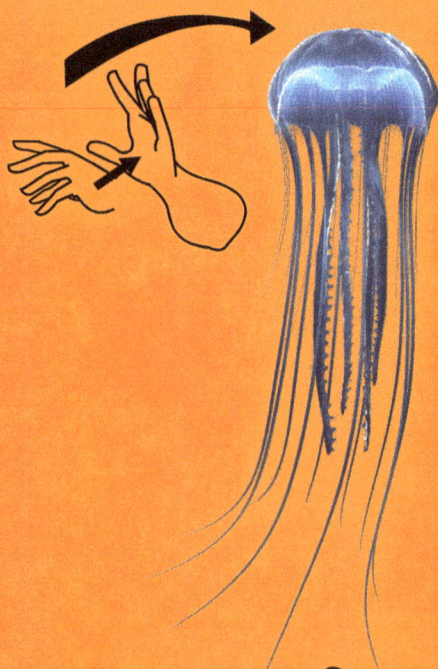

Jellyfish

Stingray

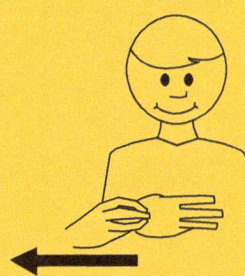

Squid

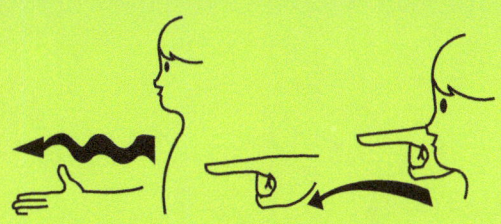

Swordfish

Catfish 27

Grasslands

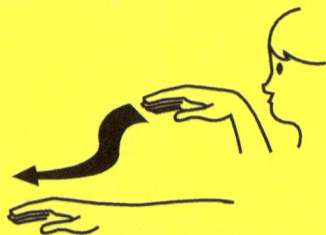

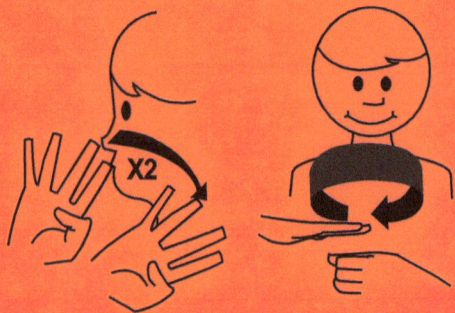

Elephant

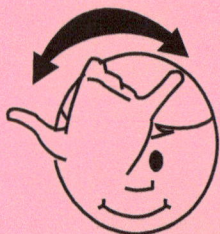

28 Buffalo

Armadillo

Tarantula

Rhinoceros

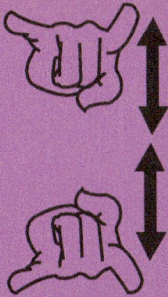

Hippopotamus

X2

Boar 29

Gazelle

Scorpion

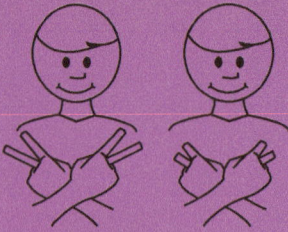

30 Koala

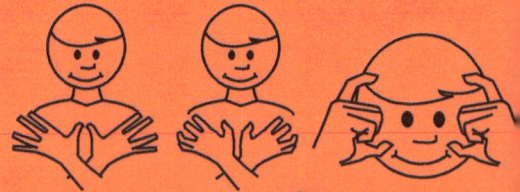

Panda

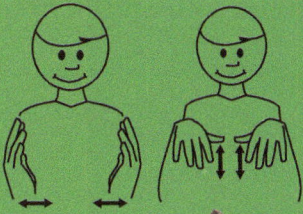

Wallaby

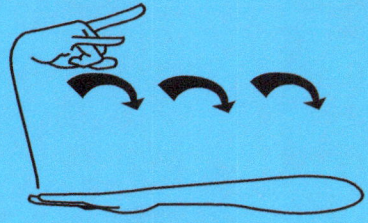

Hyena

Sloth

Lion 31

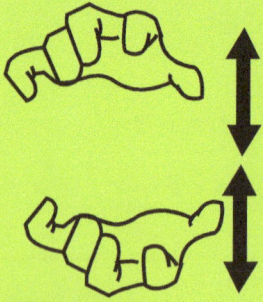

Crocodile

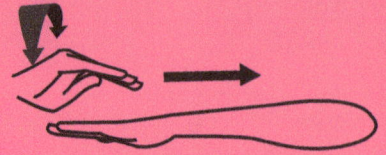

Gecko

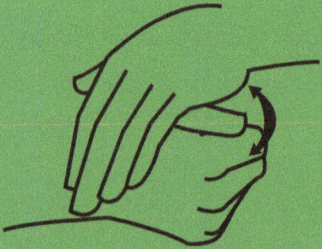

32 Tortoise

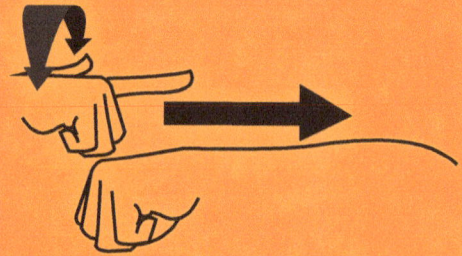

Lizard

Giraffe

Zebra

Cheetah

Mouse 33

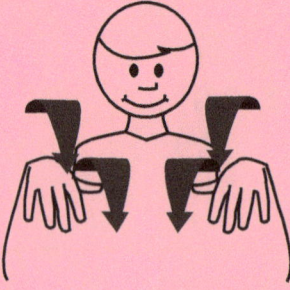

Kangaroo

Camel

34 Vulture

Wild Dog

Tasmanian Devil

Flamingo

Platypus

Tapir 35

Bugs

Grasshopper

36 Ladybug

Termite

Butterfly

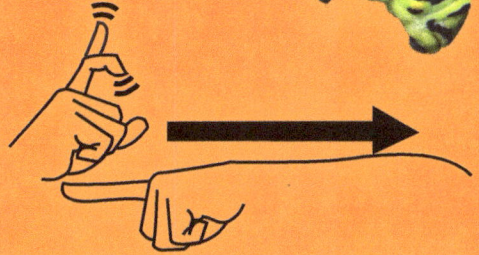

Caterpillar

Dragonfly

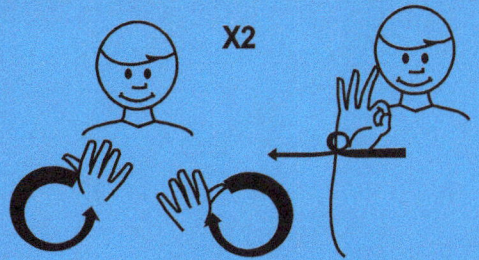

Firefly 37

Centipede

Mosquito

38 Wasp

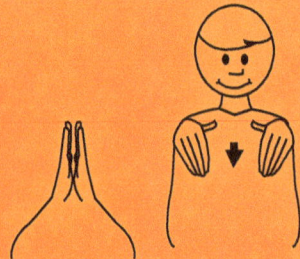

Praying Manti

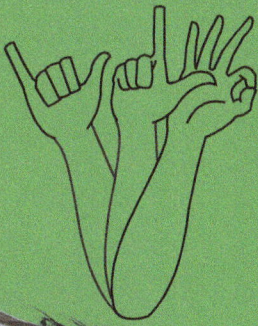

Fly

Bumble Bee

Spider

Moth 39

Equator

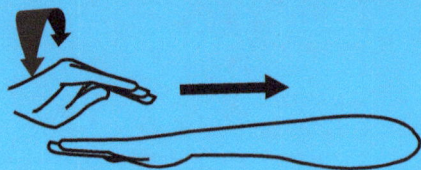

Iguana

40 Snake

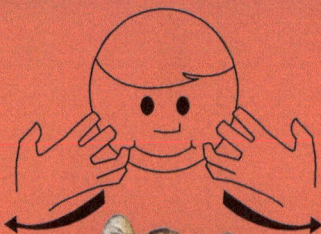

Tiger

Tree Frog

Chameleon

Parrot

Jaguar 41

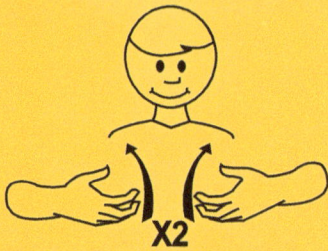

Monkey

Orangutan

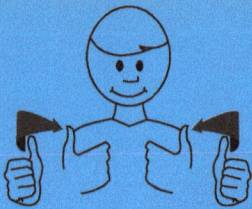

42 **Gorilla**

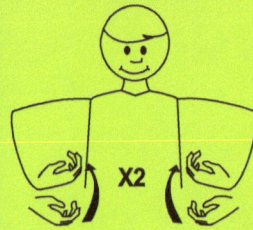

Chimpanzee

Birds

X2

X2

Woodpecker

Bluejay

Pigeon 43

Stork

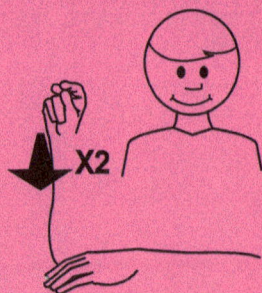

Swan

44 Pelican

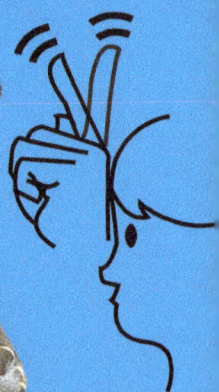

Quail

Robin

Crow

Hummingbird

Pheasant 45

activity /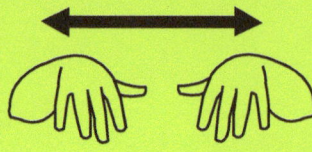

Match the following to the pictures below.

Can you find:
a cat,
a monkey,
a starfish,
a squirrel,
a duck,
a bumble bee,
an elephant,
a penguin,
and a worm?

penguin /

bumble bee /

squirrel /

elephant /

worm /

duck /

46

monkey /

cat /

starfish /

Explore other books at www.engagebooks.com

ENGAGING READERS — LEVEL T — FIRST WORDS
Available in other languages!

FARMER · TREE · APPLE · STAR
HOUSE · DOG · HAND · BALL · SHOES · TRUCK · MOON · BABY · RED · JUMP

The Toddler's **First 150 sight words** handbook

ENGAGING READERS — LEVEL T — FIRST WORDS
Available in other languages!

HELICOPTER · EXCAVATOR · FIRE TRUCK · SCHOOL BUS
TRACTOR · AMBULANCE · DUMP TRUCK · BIPLANE · BULLDOZER · PIRATE SHIP · MUSCLE CAR · TUG BOAT · POLICE CAR · TRAIN

The Toddler's **Trains planes + automobiles** and things that go handbook

ENGAGING READERS — LEVEL T — FIRST WORDS
Available in other languages!

EAGLE · CHIMPANZEE · STARFISH · DOLPHIN
ZEBRA · PANDA · DOG · TURTLE · PENGUIN · CLOWNFISH · TREE FROG · LION · BUTTERFLY · ELEPHANT

The Toddler's **First 150 animal** handbook

ENGAGING READERS — LEVEL T — FIRST WORDS
Now available in 20 languages!

NUMBERS · COLORS · SHAPES · ABCs
OPPOSITES · SIZES · FOOD · ENGINES · SOUNDS · TIME · ACTIONS · SPORTS · BODY · EMOTIONS

The Toddler's handbook
With over **100 Words** *that every kid should know*

ENGAGING READERS — LEVEL P — EARLY CONCEPTS
Includes 15 basic concepts!

ABCs · NUMBERS · COLORS · SHAPES
MUSIC · SCHOOL · MANNERS · MATCHING · BIKING · GARDENING · JOBS · ARTS · BRUSH TEETH · POTTY

The Preschooler's handbook
With over **300 Words** *that every kid should know*

ENGAGING READERS — LEVEL K — READY FOR SCHOOL
Includes 19 basic concepts!

ABCs · COLORS · MATH · SHAPES
VOWELS · TIME · SEASONS · SENSES · WEATHER · RHYMES · CALENDAR · PATTERNS · SCHOOL · CHORES

The Kindergartener's handbook
With over **300 Words** *that every kid should know*

LARGE 8.5"X11" SIZE! — LEVEL T — AGES 3 - 4
With activities throughout!

The Toddler's **WORKBOOK**
ABC 1 2 3 4 5 6 7 8 9 10 Z
Alphabet, Numbers, Shapes, Sizes, Patterns, Matching, Activities, and More!

LARGE 8.5"X11" SIZE! — LEVEL P — AGES 4 - 5
With activities throughout!

The Preschooler's **WORKBOOK** 20
A A A A a a a a 1 5 10 15 20
Alphabet, Numbers, Shapes, Sizes, Patterns, Matching, Activities, and More!

LARGE 8.5"X11" SIZE! — LEVEL K — AGES 5 - 6
With activities throughout!

The Kindergartner's **WORKBOOK**
A A a a 1 5 10 15 20
Alphabet, Numbers, Shapes, Sizes, Patterns, Matching, Activities, and More!

Have comments or suggestions?
Contact us at: alexis@engagebooks.ca

Show us how you enjoy your **#engagingreaders**. Tweet a picture to **@engagebooks** for a chance to win free prizes.

www.ingramcontent.com/pod-product-compliance
Lightning Source LLC
Chambersburg PA
CBHW040312050426
42452CB00018B/2811